LifePrints 2

ESL FOR ADULTS

Christy M. Newman

Robert Ventre Associates, Inc.

with

Allene Guss Grognet

Center for Applied Linguistics

and

JoAnn (Jodi) Crandall

University of Maryland - Baltimore County

New Readers Press

ISBN 0-88336-035-7

Copyright © 1993
New Readers Press
Publishing Division of Laubach Literacy International
Box 131, Syracuse, New York 13210-0131

Printed in the United States of America

Illustrated by Animotion, Jerry Bates, and Dick Falzoi

Cover illustrations by John D'Allaird

9 8 7 6

Table of Contents

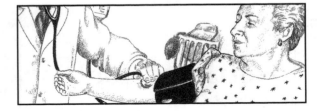

1 2 3 4 5 6 7 8 9 10 11 12

Getting a Job ■ ■ ■ ■ ■ ■ ■ ■ ■ ■ ■ ■

Looking for Work

 What's going on?

What Do They Do?

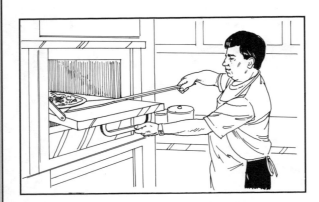

Tony Martino is from Italy.
He came to the United States
30 years ago. He makes pizzas
and sandwiches.

- **What do you call his job?**
- **What other things do you think
  he does?**

Isabel Santos is from El Salvador.
She takes money from customers
and makes change. She also uses
a computer.

- **What do you call her job?**
- **What other things do you think
  she does?**

Kim Lee is from Korea.
She serves meals to customers
at the restaurant.

- **What do you call her job?**
- **What other things do you think
  she does?**

Joon Lee is Kim's husband.
He is unemployed. He's looking
for a job.

- **Why do you think he is reading
  the newspaper?**

Isabel and Kim both work at Pizza Time. Isabel uses the computer to order supplies, but she doesn't make the meals. She can't cook. Kim serves the food to the customers. She can make the pizzas and some of the meals, but she can't use the computer.

Joon is looking for work. He can run all kinds of machines, but he can't fix the machines. He can also paint houses. He can learn how to do other things too.

A. Interview.

What can you do? What can't you do?

	Can	Can't
1. ___I___		
2. _____		
3. _____		
4. _____		
5. _____		

B. Think and talk about the questions.

1. What do you **want** to learn to do?
2. What do you think you **can** learn to do?

A. Write the answers.

1. Where will Joon apply? _____

2. Why? _____

B. Think and talk about the questions.

1. Do you ever read community bulletin boards in stores?
2. What kinds of ads do you see?

| business | painted | learn | experience | résumé |

A. Complete the sentences.

1. Joon _____ his sister's house.

2. Joon gave Mr. Bloom his _____.

3. Joon doesn't have the right _____ for the job.

4. Mr. Bloom has a painting _____.

5. Joon says he can _____ more about painting.

B. Think and talk about the questions.

1. Did Joon get the job?
2. How do you think Joon felt?
3. How would you feel?

Completing an Application

SEACOAST INDUSTRIES APPLICATION FORM
(Please print.)

Name _Lee_ _Joon_ _____

Last   First   Middle

Phone Number _(310) 427-8947_   **Social Security Number** _062-99-2814_

Are you a U.S. citizen? ☐ Yes ☑ No

If not, do you have a legal right to work in the U.S.? ☑ Yes ☐ No

Work Experience

		Job	Years at Job
1. _Chang Industries_		Machinist	1992
2. _Korean Cycling Company_		Machinist	1986 - 91

Type of Job Desired _Machine Operator_   **When You Can Start** _right away_

Availability (Circle shifts you can work.)   8 a.m.–4 p.m.   (4 p.m.–12 a.m.)   12 a.m.–8 a.m.

Joon Lee   _February 17, 1994_

Signature   Date

Fill in this form.

APPLICATION FORM
(Please print.)

Name _____

Last   First   Middle

Phone Number _____   **Social Security Number** _____

Are you a U.S. citizen? ☐ Yes ☐ No

If not, do you have a legal right to work in the U.S.? ☐ Yes ☐ No

Work Experience

		Job	Years at Job
1. _____			
Company		Job	Years at Job
2. _____			
Company		Job	Years at Job

Type of Job Desired _____   **When You Can Start** _____

Availability (Circle shifts you can work.)   8 a.m.–4 p.m.   4 p.m.–12 a.m.   12 a.m.–8 a.m.

_____   _____

Signature   Date

Seacoast Industries

Welcome to Seacoast Industries!
Seacoast Industries is a fish packaging company located in Long Beach, California, near Los Angeles.

Alberto Santana started the company in 1965 with five employees. The company now has over 200 workers.

At Seacoast Industries we clean, freeze, and package fish.

Seacoast Industries has used automated machines since 1980. With this system the fish stays fresh and tasty all the way to the customer's plate!

Seacoast Industries is now one of the leading food packagers in the country.

A. Find the information.

1. What does Seacoast Industries do? _____

2. Who started the company? _____

3. How many people worked for the company in 1965? _____

4. How many people work for Seacoast Industries today? _____

5. What kind of machines does the company use now? _____

B. Think and talk about the questions.

1. What do you think people at Seacoast Industries do?
2. Would you like to work there?

Joon's Second Interview

A. Check. ✔

Mr. Ellis asked . . .

	True	False
1. Joon about his job in Korea.	✔	
2. if Joon had a wife and children.		
3. if Joon repaired machines.		
4. why Joon left Korea.		
5. why Joon left Chang Industries.		

B. Check. ✔

Joon asked . . .

	True	False
1. about the hours of the job.		
2. about working a day shift.		
3. if Seacoast Industries has a family health plan.		
4. how much the job pays.		
5. what day he would start.		

Emi Satoh is at an interview with Mr. Ellis.

Match.

He says:		**She says:**
1. Have you ever worked in an office before?		**a.** In Torrance.
2. When did you come to the United States?		**b.** 3 p.m. to 11 p.m.
3. Where do you live now?		**c.** Yes, I have.
4. Where did you work last?		**d.** Ms. Fumiko Shoda.
5. Who was your supervisor?		**e.** In 1990.
6. What shift did you work?		**f.** At West Coast Imports, Limited.

Asking Questions

A. You are at an interview with Mr. Ellis. Write your questions.

You say:	Mr. Ellis says:
1. _What are the hours_ ?	From 7 a.m. to 3 p.m.
2. _____ ?	$300 a week.
3. _____ ?	Two weeks vacation.
4. _____ ?	Ten sick days a year.
5. _____ ?	You can start Monday at 7 a.m.

B. Think and talk about the question.

What questions do you need to ask at an interview?

Job 1:

MEAT CUTTER. P/T. Weekends. Seeking butcher with 5 years experience in food service/meat cutting. Competitive pay and benefits. Call Al at 909-5445.

Job 2:

MANAGER TRAINEE. 9-5. National Appliance Co. Training period 3–5 months. Qualified managers earn high income. Call Mr. Mitchell 599-7344.

Job 3:

OFFICE ASSISTANT. F/T person, accurate and organized. Computer exp. and good typing skills req. Downtown location. Send resume to DRA, 54474 Hollywood Blvd., L.A., 90098 ATTN: Ms. Smith.

Job 4:

$$ DRIVERS $$. For growing delivery service. Must have own car. $425-$625/wk. 12 a.m.-7 a.m. Tues.-Sat. Neat appearance. Apply in person. 78 Mechanics Alley, West L.A.

A. Check. ✔

Look at the ads.
In which job can you . . .

	1	2	3	4
1. work indoors?	✔	✔	✔	
2. get benefits?				
3. get training?				
4. work on the weekend?				
5. work at night?				

B. Write the answers.

1. Look at the job ads again. What jobs would you like? Why?

   _____

   _____

2. What jobs wouldn't you like? Why?

   _____

   _____

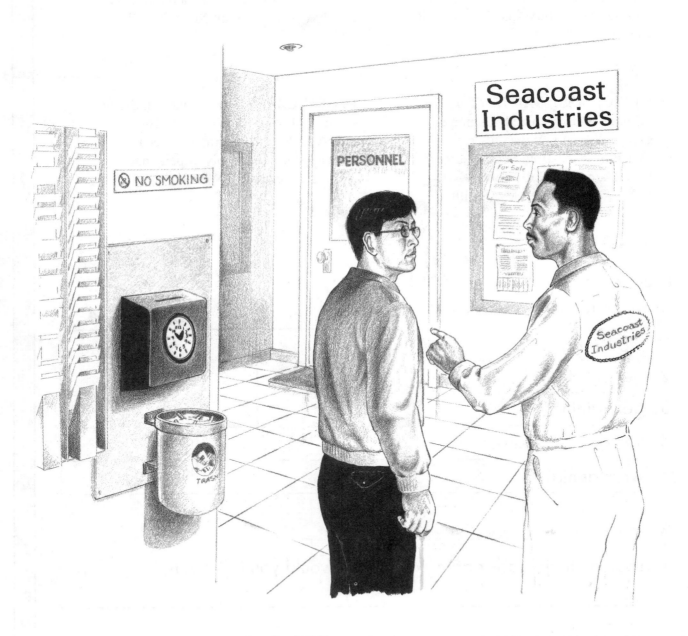

First Day on the Job

What's going on?

1. First,

2. Then,

3. Next,

4. Finally,

Think and talk about the questions.

1. How do you think Joon felt on his first day at work?
2. How did you feel on your first day at school or work?

SEACOAST INDUSTRIES   Weekly Time Card

Employee's Name Fernández   Ramón
(Please print.)   Last   First
Job Title Machine Shop Supervisor
Social Security Number   672 - 24 - 0009

EXTRA TIME					REGULAR TIME
		Feb. 21	P.M.	IN OUT	4:00
					8:00
			P.M.	IN OUT	8:30
			P.M.	IN OUT	
			P.M.	IN OUT	
		Feb. 25	P.M.	IN OUT	
			P.M.	IN OUT	
TOTAL				**TOTAL** Hours for Week	

Pay Period Ending _____

Signature _____

Choose the correct word.

First	Next
Then	Finally

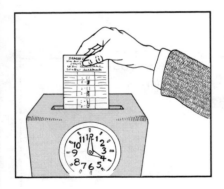

_____

_____First_____   _____   _____

Joon started his job at Seacoast Industries. He read about the company's rules in the Employee Handbook.

D. Work Shifts

Seacoast Industries is open 24 hours a day. There are three work shifts:

8:00 a.m. to 4:00 p.m.
4:00 p.m. to 12:00 midnight
12:00 midnight to 8:00 a.m.

You must be on time for your shift. You must punch in for yourself. No one else can punch in for you. If you break the rule, you may be fired.

E. Safety

You must always use caution on the job. You must obey all safety rules at work.

- Do not allow others to use your machinery or tools.
- Wear a hard hat, safety glasses, and a work uniform.

This is for your safety and the safety of your co-workers.

A. Choose the correct sentence in each pair.

1. _____ Seacoast Industries closes at night.

   _____ Seacoast Industries is open day and night.

2. _____ Employees may be fired if they do not punch in for themselves.

   _____ Employees may punch in for friends.

3. _____ Employees must pay attention to safety rules.

   _____ Employees may let other workers use their tools.

B. Think and talk about the question.

What are your rules at work?

Operating Machines

A. Complete the sentences.

1. Joon starts the machine with the _____.
   (switch/lever)

2. Then he pushes the _____ to load the packs.
   (lever/belt)

3. Joon's job is to _____ unlabeled packs.
   (remove/start)

4. He has to _____ the machine if there is a problem.
   (switch/stop)

5. Joon must _____ the bags on the shelves.
   (stack/remove)

B. Think and talk about the questions.

1. Did you understand the directions that Ramón gave to Joon?
2. What can you do if you don't understand important information?

A. Read these reasons for calling in.

1. His car won't start.

2. He has a toothache.

B. Write the reasons for calling in.

1. _____

2. _____

C. Write two more reasons for calling in.

1. _____

2. _____

Absent from Work

A. Why won't Helen be in? _____

B. Complete the conversation.

Olga Kovacs: Good morning. Seacoast Industries. May I help you?

    You: Hello. _____.

                               (Identify yourself.)

         Can I speak to _____?

                               (Give name of supervisor.)

    Olga: I'm sorry. He's not available right now. May I take a message?

    You: Yes, please tell him that _____

_____.

                               (Give message.)

    Olga: I'll be sure to give him the message.

    You: _____.

                               (End the conversation.)

What are they talking about?
Underline the correct answer.

A. 1. work 2. sports 3. friends

B. 1. family 2. shopping 3. weather

C. 1. movies 2. children 3. car problems

Safety Signs at Work

A. Look at the picture. Write the correct number on each sign.

1. Caution: Wet Floor	**2. Emergency Exit**
3. Hard Hat Area	**4. Wear Safety Glasses at All Times**

B. Write what you can say to a friend.

1. Caution: Wet Floor ___Watch out! The floor is wet.___

2. Emergency Exit _____

3. Hard Hat Area _____

4. Wear Safety Glasses at All Times _____

Memo

TO: All Seacoast Employees
FROM: Arthur Ellis
RE: Building Repairs

A construction crew will install new glass doors and windows in the factory next week. Repairs will begin on Monday morning and will continue through Thursday afternoon.

For your own safety, you should:
- use the rear entrance.
- park in the visitors' parking lot.
- use caution when walking near the building.
- cooperate with the crew members who are working in your area.

Thank you.

Check. ✔

Seacoast employees . . .

	True	False	Doesn't Say
1. can have lunch with crew members.			
2. can use the front door on Friday morning.			
3. can't park in the employees' parking lot.			
4. can park anywhere.			
5. can't walk near the building.			

Making the Connection

Joon started his new job in February. He is a machine operator at Seacoast Industries, and he packages frozen fish. He likes his job, and he likes the people at the factory too. He says that everyone at Seacoast is very friendly.

Joon's first day at Seacoast was very busy. First he met his new supervisor and got his uniform. Then he learned how to punch in and how to operate a new machine. He also learned about the company's safety rules. Finally, he met some co-workers.

Write about yourself.

I have a job. I am a _____

at _____.

I started my job in _____.

I like _____ at my job.

I don't like _____ at my job.

My first day at work was _____.

I learned _____.

Then _____.

Finally, _____.

123456789101112

Making Choices about Money ■ ■ ■

Payday

What's going on?

Reading a Pay Stub

SEACOAST INDUSTRIES	Check No. 18976	Week Ending 3/4/94

Lee, Joon
Employee No. 212
SSN: 062-99-2814

Base Rate
of Salary: 7.00   Amount of Check: 214.47

Gross Pay	Taxes	Deductions	Net Pay	Description	Taxes/ Ded.	Year- to-Date
280.00	42.20	23.33	214.47	Federal Taxes	24.49	48.98
				State Taxes	9.71	19.42
				Health Insurance	23.33	46.66
				FICA	8.00	16.00

Description	Hours	Earnings	Year-to-Date
Regular	40.00	280.00	560.00
Vacation	2		4 hours
Overtime	0		0
Sick	2		4 hours

Underline the correct answer.

1. Joon gets paid every (week, other week, month).

2. Gross pay is (more than, less than, the same as) net pay.

3. His weekly gross pay is ($214.47, $280.00, $560.00).

4. Joon's biggest deduction is (federal tax, state tax, health insurance).

5. This is Joon's (first, second, third) paycheck.

The Lee Family Monthly Budget

Income:

Take-home pay:	Kim :		$540.00
	Joon :		$857.88
	Total monthly income:		**$1,397.88**
Monthly Expenses:	Rent	$425	
	Utilities	$185	
	Bus Pass (Joon)	$ 45	
	Phone	$ 25	
		$680	$680.00
Other Expenses:	Food	$500	
	Medical	$ 32	
	Miscellaneous	$ 50	
		$582	$582.00
	Total monthly expenses:		**$1,262.00**
	Balance:		**$135.88**

A. Write the answers.

How much . . .

1. do Kim and Joon take home every month? $_____

2. more does Joon make every month than Kim? $_____

3. are their medical costs? $_____

4. can they save each month? $_____

B. Think and talk about the questions.

1. What are your miscellaneous expenses?

2. How do you usually spend your paycheck?

Need or Want?

Joon and Kim just got their paychecks. Joon wants to buy Kim a beautiful new dress. Kim doesn't want a new dress. She says, "We need to buy Han a new jacket. His jacket is torn." Joon is sad because he wants to get Kim something nice, but he knows that Kim is right. She doesn't need a new dress now.

List the things that you . . .

need.   **want but don't need.**

_____   _____

_____   _____

_____   _____

_____   _____

_____   _____

S-Mart Spring Specials

$29.99

Major nonstick iron
- 53 self-clean vents
- fabric guide
- 12-ft. cord

$29.98

$69.00

Fargo's 10-cup coffeemaker • digital
- brews a cup a minute

TT&D 2-line phone
- 3-party conference calling

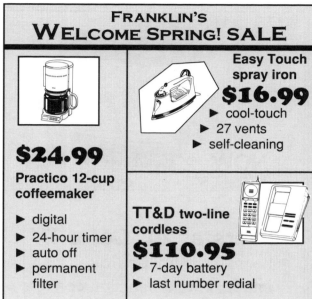

FRANKLIN'S WELCOME SPRING! SALE

$24.99

Practico 12-cup coffeemaker
- ▶ digital
- ▶ 24-hour timer
- ▶ auto off
- ▶ permanent filter

Easy Touch spray iron

$16.99
- ▶ cool-touch
- ▶ 27 vents
- ▶ self-cleaning

TT&D two-line cordless

$110.95
- ▶ 7-day battery
- ▶ last number redial

A. List the special features of the items above.

	S-Mart	Franklin's
1. iron		
2. telephone		
3. coffeemaker.....		

B. Think and talk about the questions.

1. What do you look for when you buy items like those listed above?
2. How do you decide if an item is a good buy?

What's the Better Buy?

SAVE $30

NOW $349.⁹⁹ *Reg. $379.*⁹⁹

Silverstar 20" Color TV
- Remote control operates image/sound/function controls
- 181 channels • On-screen display
- Ultra-sharp picture
- Stereo sound

SAVE $40

NOW $199.⁹⁹ *Reg. $239.*⁹⁹

Focus 19" Color TV
- Chromacolor contrast picture tube
- Portable
- 68-channel capacity with programmable channel skip

A. Check. ✔

Which TV . . .

	Silverstar	Focus
1. is smaller?		
2. is more expensive?		
3. has more channels?		
4. has a better discount?		
5. has more features?		

B. Think and talk about the question.
Which TV would you buy? Why?

Put the pictures in order.

_____

_____

__1__

_____

_____

Ways to Pay

cash

check or
money order

credit card

	Advantages +	Disadvantages −
	You only spend what you have. You don't pay any extra costs.	You may have to wait to buy some things.
	You only spend what you have. You have a record of your purchases.	You may have to wait to buy some things. You may have to pay extra service charges.
	You can buy things before you have the money for them. You can buy things in an emergency.	You may have to pay extra service charges and interest costs. You may have to pay a fee to use the credit card.

Check. ✔

How do you pay . . .	Cash	Check or Money Order	Credit Card
1. for groceries?			
2. for a new television?			
3. for gas for your car?			
4. your telephone bill?			
5. for a candy bar?			
6. _____ ?			

Royal's Credit Card Application

Account to be billed in the name of __Monroe Bonner__

Billing Address __26 High Street, Westland, CA 90600__

Bank __Westland Savings Bank__

Account no. __12218-6453__ __12249-034__
       Checking   Savings

Employer __Seacoast Industries__ Years there __3__

Monthly income __$1,500__ Monthly rent or mortgage __$700__

No. of dependents __2__ Own home _____ Rent __✓__

Name, address, and relationship of nearest relative not living with you
__Samuel Bonner, 4 Byville Rd., Compton, CA 90221 (Father)__

List other credit cards and outstanding balances below.

1. __Charge-All $250__   2. __S-Mart Card -0-__
3. _____   4. _____

List credit references below. (Include all debts now owed.)

Company and address	Acct no.	Balance
1. Westland Savings Bank – Auto loan 3 Stanhope Road, Westland, CA 90600	2-1881	$1,500
2.		

A. Write the answers.

1. What is the **first** thing Monroe should do with his new credit card?

   _____

2. When can Monroe use his credit card?

   _____

3. What should Monroe do if he loses the card?

   _____

ROYAL'S
TERMS AND CONDITIONS OF SALE

1. All parts of this product are guaranteed for 1 year. Royal will repair or replace the product if material or workmanship is defective. This guarantee does not cover deliberate damage, theft, or unapproved repairs.

2. Returned Checks: A $15.00 fee is charged for each returned check.

ROYAL'S RETURN POLICY

If you are not happy with your purchase, please return it within 30 days. Bring your receipt. We will repair the product, exchange it, issue a refund, or credit your account.

You bought something at Royal's two weeks ago.
You bring it back to the store.

If you say. . .   *Royal's will . . .*

	repair the item.	exchange the item.	refund your money.	give you a credit.
1. My TV needs a new switch.	✔			
2. I don't want this. I'd like my cash back.				
3. My son already bought one. Please credit my account.				
4. This one doesn't work. I'd like the same model.				
5. Please fix this radio.				
6. This one is defective. Give me one that costs the same.				
7. My wife doesn't want this. Please give me my money back.				

Kim Lee went to Toy Town to buy her son, Han, a bicycle. She looked at all the bikes. Then she saw a nice, red bike. She knew that Han would love it. Kim didn't have enough money. She only had $25 and the bike cost $85. She thought about using a credit card but decided not to.

Kim went to the layaway counter at Toy Town. She asked the woman to put the bicycle on layaway. Kim gave the woman $25 and filled out a form. She still owes $60 for the bicycle. Kim can bring the bike home when she pays the rest of the money.

Write a story that answers these questions about something you bought.

1. What store did you go to?
2. What did you want to buy?
3. How much did it cost?
4. Did you have enough money?
5. How did you pay for it?

I went to _____. I wanted to buy

_____. I saw a _____.

It cost_____. I _____ enough money.

I bought it _____.

Getting Around

What's going on?
How do you get around?

A. Take notes.

Monday, May _____ at _____.
Bring:

B. Think and talk about the questions.

1. Do you have a driver's license?
2. If you do have a license, what did you do to get it?
3. How does someone get a driver's license in your native country?

Car Insurance

A. Complete the sentences.

1. This is Isabel's first _____.

2. Compulsory coverage pays for your _____ bills if you are in an accident.

3. This insurance also pays for medical expenses to anyone who is _____ by your car.

4. You don't _____ to buy optional coverage if you don't want to.

5. _____ coverage pays for most of the damage to your car.

B. Think and talk about the questions.

1. Is buying insurance a good idea? Why or why not?

2. What other kinds of insurance can you buy?

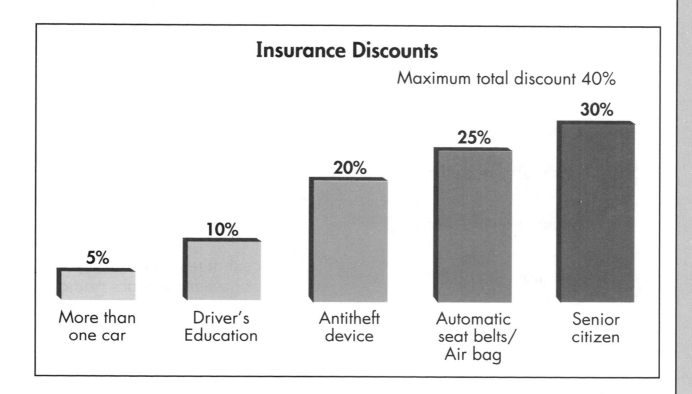

Insurance Discounts

Maximum total discount 40%

5% — More than one car
10% — Driver's Education
20% — Antitheft device
25% — Automatic seat belts/Air bag
30% — Senior citizen

A. Choose the correct sentence in each pair.

1. _____ Driver's Education saves you money on your insurance.
   _____ Driver's Education saves you more money than having automatic seat belts.

2. _____ You save money with all seat belts.
   _____ You save money with automatic seat belts.

3. _____ Antitheft devices save you more money than automatic seat belts.
   _____ Automatic seat belts or air bags save you more money than antitheft devices.

4. _____ If you have more than one car, you get the biggest discount.
   _____ Senior citizens get the biggest discount.

B. Think and talk about the questions.

1. Why do you think senior citizens get a discount on insurance?
2. Why is there a discount for a car with an antitheft device?

Reading a Driver's Manual

Traffic Signs

Traffic signs tell you about traffic rules, special warnings, where you are, and how to get to other places. The shape of a traffic sign gives you important information.

signs that give traffic rules

signs that give a warning

signs that tell you there is a railroad

signs that tell you to stop

signs that tell you to slow down, look, and be prepared to stop

signs that tell you where you are or where you are going

Write the correct information on each sign.

STOP	SPEED LIMIT 50	RR
San Diego 17	ROAD WORK	YIELD

1.

2.

3.

4.

5.

6.

Parking Regulations

Parking in "No Parking" areas can cause accidents.
The law does not permit parking your vehicle:

1. in a crosswalk.
2. within an intersection.
3. on a sidewalk.
4. within 10 feet of a hydrant.
5. in front of a driveway or a handicapped ramp.
6. within a posted bus stop.

Which regulation is being broken? Write the number.

———

———

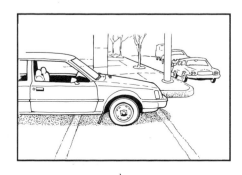

1

———

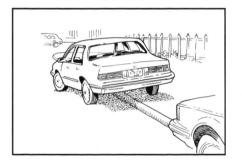

———

———

Applying for a License

Fill in the form.

Application for Driver's License

1. Name _
       Last   First   M.I.

2. Date of birth _ _ / _ _ / _ _   3. Sex ☐   ☐
            Month   Day   Year   Male   Female

4. Address _
           No. and Street

5. City _

6. State _

7. County/Zip Code _

8. Height _ ' _ _ "

9. Eye Color _ _ _ _ _ _

10. Do you have a driver's license in another state or country? ☐   ☐
                                                           Yes   No

    If you checked yes, where? _ _ _ _ _ _ _ _ _ _ _ _ _ _ _ _ _ _ _

A. Draw Johnny's route.

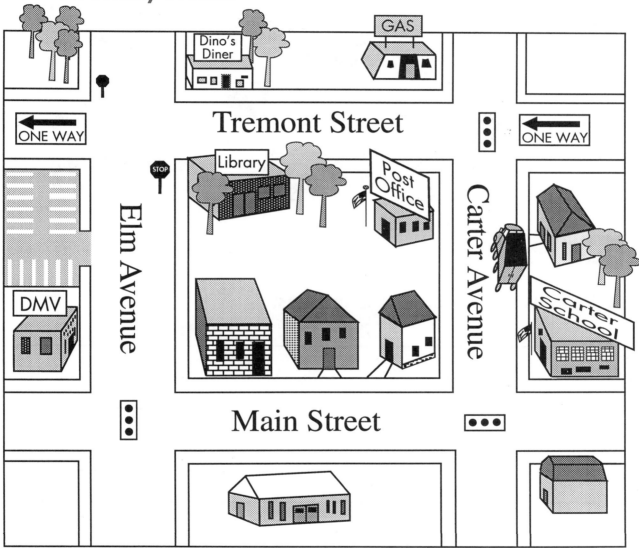

Tremont Street

Elm Avenue

Carter Avenue

Main Street

ONE WAY

ONE WAY

STOP

DMV

Library

Post Office

Dino's Diner

GAS

Carter School

B. Think and talk about the questions.

1. Are drivers in the United States good drivers? Why? Why not?

2. Do drivers in your native country drive more or less carefully than drivers in the United States?

3. How do you drive?

Getting Pulled Over

A. Put these pictures in order. Write the numbers.

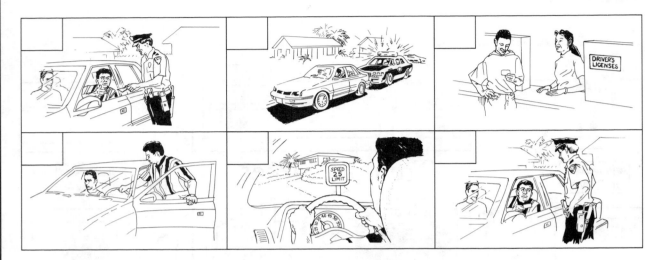

B. Write sentences about the pictures.

1. _____
2. _____
3. _____
4. _____
5. _____
6. _____

C. Think and talk about the questions.

1. Why do you think Johnny was angry?
2. Why do you think Tony drove home from the Department of Motor Vehicles?
3. What should Tony do about his speeding ticket?
4. Have you ever received a speeding ticket?

UNIFORM TRAFFIC CITATION

COURT DOCKET NO.	DATE CITATION WRITTEN 5/9/94	POLICE DEPARTMENT Long Beach	☑ OWNER ☐ OPERATOR	1571023

NAME (Last, First, Initial) Martino, Tony	DATE OF BIRTH 6-4-44	VEHICLE OWNER (IF DIFFERENT)

ADDRESS 585 La Brea Ave.	ADDRESS

CITY/TOWN Westland	STATE CA	ZIP 90600	CITY/TOWN	STATE ZIP

LICENSE NO. A2W-84659	STATE CA	LIC. EXP. DATE 5-4-96	ROAD: ☑DRY ☐WET ☐SNOW AREA: ☑SETTLED ☐RURAL	NO. LANES 2

REGISTRATION NO. 986-95-0052-374	STATE CA	EXP. DATE 8-95	MAKE & TYPE Dodge Omni	YEAR 90	COLOR Bl	TRAFFIC ☐HVY ☐MED ☑LT	ROAD DIVIDED ☐YES ☑NO

DATE OF VIOLATION 5-9-94	LOCATION OF VIOLATION Rutford & Main Street	TIME 4:30	☐AM ☑PM	ACCIDENT ☐YES ☑NO

OFFENSE
A. ☐ CRIM
   ☐ CIVIL

B. ☑CIVIL SPEEDING	35 MPH IN A 25 MPH ZONE	☑CLOCKED ☐RADAR ☐ESTIMATED	TOTAL AMOUNT DUE $50.00	CHAPT. SECT

NOTICE TO VIOLATOR SEE REVERSE SIDE OF THIS CITATION FOR IMPORTANT INFORMATION ON YOUR RIGHTS AND DUTIES REGARDING THIS CITATION.

OFFICER CERTIFIES COPY GIVEN TO VIOLATOR
X *Paul MacKennau*

BADGE NO.
9874

☑IN HAND
☐BY MAIL

VIOLATOR ACKNOWLEDGES RECEIPT OF CITATION
X *Tony Bonzani*

VIOLATOR COPY

A. Check. ✔

	True	False
1. It was raining.		
2. Tony owns the car.		
3. Tony must pay a $50 fine.		
4. Tony was driving on a highway.		
5. Tony was driving in the afternoon.		
6. Tony was in an accident.		

B. Think and talk about the question.

1. What do you think will happen to Tony's insurance rates?

Making the Connection

F & G Supermarket

Johnny was driving to the supermarket. He was paying attention to all the traffic signs and following all the traffic rules. Then he pulled into the parking lot and came too close to the car in the next space. He hit the car and dented the fender. He didn't know the owner of the car, but he wanted to explain what happened.

Imagine that this happened to you.
Write a note.

- Tell what happened.
- Tell who you are.
- Tell how to reach you.

I'm sorry that

I'm
My number is

1 2 3 4 5 6 7 8 9 10 11 12

Having a Good Time ■ ■ ■ ■ ■ ■ ■

Plans for the 4th of July

What are they going to do?
What do you like to do on holidays?

Things to Do

Monday

Concert featuring
Jamie Jive and the Jazz Notes
Tickets $20   6 p.m.
Call for details: 480-3232
The Greek Theatre at Griffith Park

Fourth of July Festival
Exposition Park
Free music, dancing, and fireworks!
6 p.m. to midnight

Olympic Basketball Team Exhibition
Tickets $5/Free to students
Pauley Pavilion/UCLA
4 to 6 p.m.

Mexican Festival
Crafts, food, music, dancing
Noon to 5:30 p.m.
Olivera Street

July 4th Parade
Floats, bands, music
Parade begins at 10 a.m.
Olivera Street to City Hall

Benefit for City Hospital
Downtown Cinema
Showing *"Yankee Doodle Dandy"*
4 p.m., 6 p.m., 8 p.m.
Tickets $50 a pair, Senior Citizens $10

Isabel and her friend, Stefan, are going out on a date. They're planning what to do. Isabel likes sports, parades, music, and dancing. She doesn't like to go to the movies. Stefan likes music, dancing, movies, and concerts. Stefan works until 5:00 p.m. Neither Isabel nor Stefan have a lot of money to spend.

A. Complete this chart.

Things to Do	Time	Cost
1. *Concert*	6 p.m.	$20
2.		
3.		
4.		
5.		
6.		

B. Think and talk about the questions.

1. What do you think Isabel and Stefan are going to do on the 4th of July?
2. What do you like to do in your free time?

A. Listen.

B. What are they saying?

The Company Picnic

Seacoast Picnic

Morning
Games for kids
Volleyball
Kite flying

Lunch: 11 a.m.–1 p.m.
Hamburgers
Hot dogs
Barbecued chicken
Fish
Corn on the cob
Watermelon

Afternoon
Soccer
Talent show
Sing-along

Joon and his family arrived at the Seacoast picnic in the morning. Monroe, Althea, and Jody were there also. While Han and Jody played games, Joon, Monroe, and Althea played volleyball. Kim went off to fly a kite. Then they all had lunch. In the afternoon, while Kim, Althea, and Jody were in the talent show, Joon, Monroe, and Han played soccer. It was a great day for everyone.

Think and talk about the questions.

1. In your native country, are there company parties?

2. What are some reasons for company parties in your native country?

What do you like to do?

_____
your name

_____
your partner's name

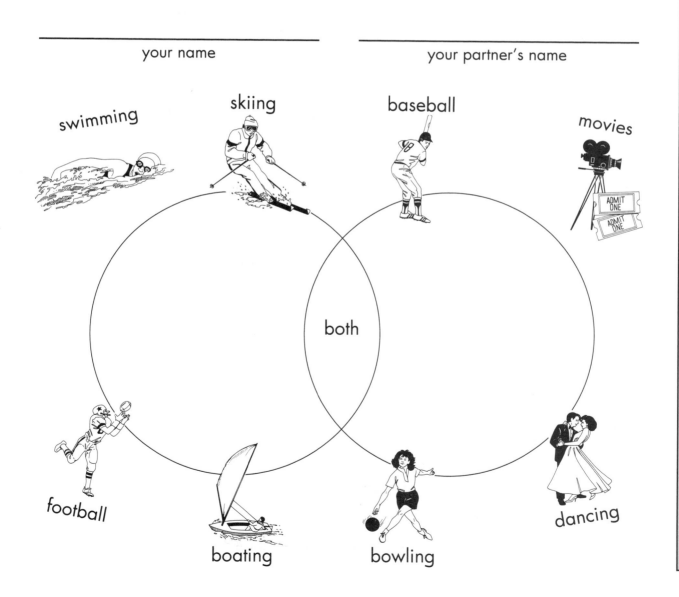

swimming · skiing · baseball · movies

both

football · boating · bowling · dancing

Tony and Johnny are going to visit Tony's sister, Tessa, at her home by the lake. Tony can't wait to spend some time away from the city. Johnny is looking forward to seeing his cousins. Both Tony and Johnny like to visit Tessa and her family. They always have a good time there.

A. Listen to the conversation.

What did Johnny forget?

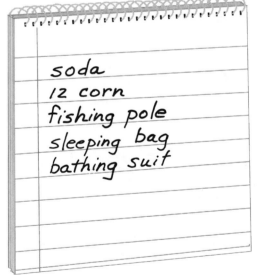

soda
12 corn
fishing pole
sleeping bag
bathing suit

B. Think and talk about the questions.

1. What else would you bring on this trip?
2. Do you ever take pets on trips with you?
3. What do you like to do on the weekend?
4. What kind of places do you like to visit?
5. Who do you like to spend time with on weekends?

Educational and Fun

Discover Waters of the World!

Thrill Rides for All Members of the Family!

Whale and Sea Lion Shows
10:00, 12:00, 2:00, 4:00

Aquarium
Over 1,000 kinds of fish

Marine Animal Exhibits
Hands-on activities for kids and adults

Wild River Rides
Daily (Reservations Required)

Water Slides
All kinds for all sizes

Wacky Wave Pool
Constantly moving, constantly crazy . . . and fun

Open Daily		Adults: $15.95
Monday – Friday	9:30 – 5:00	Children (12 and under): $10.95
Saturday & Sunday	9:30 – 8:00	Children under 2: FREE

Aunt Tessa took everyone to Waters of the World.

A. What do you think Johnny will do?

Write three things and tell why.

1. _____
2. _____
3. _____

B. Think and talk about the questions.

1. What would you do at Waters of the World?
2. Have you ever been to a place like Waters of the World? What did you do there?

A. Interview.

What season do you like? Why?

Name	Season	Why?
1.		
2.		
3.		
4.		

B. Think and talk about the questions.

1. What are the seasons in your native country?
2. Do you ever take vacations?
3. When do you like to take vacations?

1. Aunt Tessa is short and pretty. Uncle Sal is tall and handsome.

2. Johnny is thin. He caught a long, skinny fish.

3. Aunt Tessa's dog, Rolf, is ugly and strong. He's very friendly.

4. The lake was beautiful and calm.

5. The kids were loud and noisy. They were busy all weekend. They got wet and dirty.

6. The food was very good. The homemade cake was delicious.

A. Describe these people.

B. Think and talk about the questions.

1. Describe yourself to a partner.
2. Describe other people you know.

A Holiday Weekend

summer	picnic	delicious	much	free
happy	beautiful	busy	noisy	

Complete the sentences. Use each word only one time.

1. The 4th of July is a _____ holiday.

2. Joon, Kim, and Han went to the Seacoast Industries_____.

3. The Bonner family was also there. There were many things going on so it was a _____ day for everyone.

4. The food they had was _____. But Han ate too_____ watermelon and got a stomachache.

5. Isabel and Stefan went to a _____ festival in the park.

6. The music and dancing made them feel _____.

7. The fireworks were very _____, but they were also _____.

July 8, 1994

Dear Gerry,

Uncle Sal and Aunt Tessa invited Dad and me to the lake. We spent the 4th of July there. Richie and I caught 10 fish! Big ones too! We had a great time.

We're going back next month. Aunt Tessa says your family will be there too. You sure have a long drive from Cleveland, don't you?

Did you hear? I got my license. Next time, I'll drive to your house.

I can't wait to see you!

Your cousin,
Johnny

Write a letter to a relative or friend.

_____
(date)

Dear _____,

Guess what? _____

_____

_____

I hope that _____

_____

_____

_____,

_____
(your signature)

Verbs: Past Tense

Verb	Past Tense
call	call**ed**
move	mov**ed**
watch	watch**ed**
paint	paint**ed**
work	work**ed**
plan	plan**ned**
study	stud**ied**

Johnny **studied** for his driver's test.
He **passed** the test yesterday.

The workers **didn't finish** the job last
night. They **finished** today.

Did Olga **work** yesterday?
No, she **didn't**. She **called** in sick.

start	operate	stay	plan	work	move

A. Complete the sentences. Use the past tense of the verbs above.

1. *Ramón:* "Mr. Ellis says that you _____ in a factory before."

2. *Joon:* "Yes, in a bicycle factory. I _____ a lot of different machines there."

3. *Ramón:* "Was that your first job?"

   Joon: "Yes, and I _____ with that company for five years. When did you start to work here at Seacoast Industries?"

4. *Ramón:* "I _____ here about six years ago. I never _____ to stay here so long."

5. *Joon:* "Did your family come to the United States with you?"

   Ramón: "Not at first. They just _____ here last year."

B. What did Joon do after work yesterday? You make up the sentences.

Verb	Past Tense
be	was/were
do	did
have	had
go	went
see	saw
get	got
take	took

Verb	Past Tense
write	wrote
give	gave
begin	began
feel	felt
speak	spoke
buy	bought
cost	cost

Tony **bought** a car.
It **cost** $2,500.

Tony **didn't see** the stop sign.
He **got** a traffic ticket.

Did you **see** the game?
Where **did** you **go?**

A. Complete the sentences.

1. *Kim:* "Where did you go for vacation?"
   Tony: "Johnny and I _____ to my sister's for a few days."
2. *Kim:* "Did Johnny have a good time?"
   Tony: "Oh, he _____ a great time!"
3. *Kim:* "Did you see anything special?"
   Tony: "I think we _____ everything at Waters of the World."
4. *Kim:* "There are some great rides there. Did you take any of them?"
   Tony: "Sure. We _____ lots of rides. But we didn't _____
   the Wild River Ride."

B. Make up a sentence for each picture, using the past tense of the verbs.

go to a picnic	see the fireworks	have a party

What did everyone do last weekend?

1. The Lees _____.

2. Olga _____.

3. Isabel and Stefan _____.

Verbs: Past Continuous Tense

Past Continuous Tense			
I He She	**was driving.**	We You They	**were driving.**

Past Continuous Tense	Past Tense
Was Tony **driving** the car? He **wasn't watching** the signs.	**Did** Tony **drive** home? He **didn't stop** at the light.

A. Identify the tense.

Example: Everyone **was working** at the restaurant.

	Past Continuous	Past
Example	✔	
1. Then the lights went off.		
2. Kim was serving two customers.		
3. She didn't spill anything in the dark.		
4. Tony burned his hand.		
5. Was he making a pizza?		
6. Kim put candles on the tables.		

B. Complete the sentences. Use the past continuous tense.

1. Isabel _____ (prepare) accounts on the computer.

2. The customers _____ (eat) their dinners.

3. Tony _____ (cook) some vegetables.

4. Kim _____ (talk) to some customers.

Adjective	Comparative	Adjective	Comparative
small	small**er**	pretty	prett**ier**
cheap	cheap**er**	good	**better**
large	larg**er**	bad	**worse**
big	big**ger**	expensive	**more** expensive
			less expensive

Examples: This television is too **small.** Do you have anything **larger?**
These shoes are very **expensive.** Do you have anything **less expensive?**
The baseball game was **exciting.** It was **more exciting** than the parade.

A. Underline the comparative adjectives.

1. The sale at Franklin's is bigger than at S-Mart.
2. Franklin's is more expensive.
3. S-Mart is more crowded than Franklin's during sales.
4. Franklin's has a better selection than S-Mart.
5. S-Mart is closer than Franklin's.

B. Write the comparative adjective.

1. *Althea:* "Look at this. The prices are a lot _____ (cheap) at S-Mart than at Franklin's."

2. *Olga:* "I like S-Mart's prices, but that store is _____ (noisy) than Franklin's."

3. *Althea:* "Yes, but S-Mart has _____ (good) buys. That's for sure."

4. *Olga:* "Well, the service is _____ (fast) at Franklin's than at S-Mart."

5. *Althea:* "I don't know. I think the salesclerks are _____ (nice) at S-Mart."

6. *Olga:* "Well, I feel _____ (comfortable) at Franklin's. I'm going shopping there this weekend."

Modals: *Can, Could, Would, Should*

Meaning	Modal	Example
to express ability or possibility	**can, could**	Tony **can** cook pizzas. Monroe **could** use his car. Joon **couldn't** drive to work yesterday.
to offer assistance, to ask for assistance	**can, could, would**	**Can** you help me? **Could** I get you something to drink? **Would** you like anything to eat?
to give advice, to ask for advice	**should**	When **should** we leave for the picnic? Tony **shouldn't** drive so fast.

A. Underline the correct modal.

1. *Joon:* "Monroe, I **can't/shouldn't** find any blank time cards."

2. *Monroe:* "You **would/should** speak to Olga. She has some near her desk."

3. *Joon:* "Olga, **could/should** you give me a time card? There aren't any next to the time clock."

4. *Olga:* "Here you are. **Would/Should** you put out some extra ones for me?"

5. *Joon:* "Sure. I **would/can** take them right out to the time clock."

B. Complete the sentences. Use a modal that fits.

1. *Ramón:* "These boxes _____ be blocking this door."

2. *Joon:* "_____ you like me to move them?"

3. *Ramón:* "That's all right. I think I _____ get them."

4. *Joon:* "OK. You _____ put them over there, next to the machines."

5. *Ramón:* "You know, they're all empty. Maybe we _____ just throw them out."

1 2 3 4 5 6 7 8 9 10 11 12
Wash and Wear ■ ■ ■ ■ ■ ■ ■ ■

Does It Fit?

What's going on?
What are they thinking?

Looking Their Best

Monroe, Althea, and Jody are going to a wedding. They want to look their best. Last week, they looked in their closets. They wanted to see what they could wear.

Monroe tried on his best suit and it didn't fit. He needs a new suit. Althea decided to wear her pink suit, but her best blouse has a large stain on it. She loves this blouse and she's very upset about the stain. Jody tried on her best dress and it didn't fit. She needs a new dress. They all decide to go shopping.

Think and talk about the questions.

1. Why are Monroe and Jody getting new clothes?
2. What can Althea do?
3. What would you do?

Monroe and Althea talk about several different stores:

Royal's   **FRANCIE'S FASHIONS**   J. Taylor's   **Dandelion Shop**

A. Write the answers.

Where will they go to look for clothes?

Monroe _____

Althea _____

Jody _____

B. Think and talk about the questions.

1. How do Monroe and Althea decide where to go?
2. How do you decide where to buy clothes?
3. What kinds of stores do you see in a mall?
4. Where do you buy clothes in your town?

Looking through the Racks

Monroe, Althea, and Jody are looking at the men's suits. Jody thinks the checked ones are nice. Althea prefers the brown tweed one. But Monroe really likes the navy blue suit and it's the style he wants. Monroe says, "Solid colors are more practical." He thinks this is the suit he wants to buy.

Monroe looks at the label on the suit. It's a wool suit, and that's what he wants. He doesn't like rayon blends. Monroe wants to keep this suit for a long time, so he wants to make sure that it will really last!

Then Monroe looks at the price tag. He can't believe his eyes. $499! It must be a mistake! But it isn't. The suit is much too expensive, so Monroe is going to look in Royal's Discount Store.

A. Answer these questions.

1. What kind of suit does Monroe like? _____

2. Why isn't he going to buy it? _____

3. Where can Monroe buy a cheaper suit? _____

B. Think and talk about the questions.

1. What do you need to think about when you buy clothes?

2. What kinds of clothes do you like?

A. Complete the sentences.

1. Monroe's suit size is a 43 _____.
                            (short/long)

2. Monroe wants a _____ suit.
                     (business/casual)

3. Wool blends are _____ fabrics.
                       (delicate/durable)

4. Monroe wasn't looking for a _____.
                                  (blend/style)

5. Monroe also likes the _____.
                            (price/fitting room)

B. How much will the suit cost?

_____

Choosing a Shirt

Check. ✔

	True	False
1. The blue shirt is the wrong shade for the suit.		
2. Cotton never shrinks.		
3. Althea likes to iron.		
4. "Irregular" means not perfect.		
5. Washable blends are hard to take care of.		
6. Monroe wants a shirt with long sleeves.		

Choose the correct sentence in each pair.

1. ____ Jody wears a size 8.

   ____ Jody wears a size 6.

2. ____ The dress will shrink more than 6%.

   ____ The dress will shrink up to 6%.

3. ____ You must take the dress to a dry cleaner.

   ____ You can wash the dress in a washer.

4. ____ You should wash the dress in warm water.

   ____ You should wash the dress in cold water.

5. ____ You can iron the dress.

   ____ You cannot iron the dress.

What's Important to You?

Monroe always looks for sales when he goes shopping. He hates to pay full price for anything. When he buys clothes, he wants good material that will not wear out quickly. He also wants to look good, so he looks for nice styles.

When Althea goes shopping, she looks for the same things that Monroe looks for. But she also wants materials that are easy to take care of. She doesn't like to iron, so she doesn't like to buy materials that wrinkle easily, like cotton.

The only thing that is important to Jody is style. She wants to look good all the time. She doesn't care about the price or if the material is durable and strong or if it's easy or difficult to care for. She just wants to look good!

Interview.
What's important to you?

	Easy Care	Good Price	Nice Style	Durable Fabric
1. Monroe		✓	✓	✓
2. Althea	✓	✓	✓	✓
3. Jody			✓	
4.				
5.				
6.				
7.				
8.				
Totals				

A. Complete the sentences.

1. Althea is looking for a blouse with _____ sleeves.

2. The buttons are on the _____.

3. The _____ that Althea sees are too fancy.

4. The salesclerk doesn't think that the other stores would have the _____ blouse.

5. Althea decided to try to remove the _____.

B. Think and talk about the questions.

1. What would you do if you were Althea?

2. Have you ever had an unsuccessful shopping trip?

Removing the Stain

Althea used this guide to help her remove the stain from her blouse.

Stain Removal Guide
for Washable Clothes*

	Blood	Rinse or soak in cold water right away.
	Gum	Rub with ice to make gum hard. Scrape off.
	Fruit	Soak in cool water right away. Mix a little hot water and a few drops of ammonia. Wait 15 to 30 minutes. Wash in cold water.**
	Ink	Spray with hair spray. Sponge the stain right away.***

* Do not use with clothes that must be dry-cleaned.
** Do not use soap on fruit stains. Soap will set stains.
*** Permanent (indelible) ink cannot be removed.

Check. ✔

What do you need to remove . . .

	Hot/Warm Water	Cool/Cold Water	Ice	Hair Spray	Ammonia
1. blood?					
2. gum?					
3. fruit?					
4. ink?					

Jody did the wash today.

She used too much hot water.

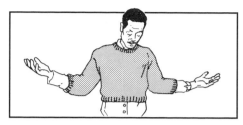

The sweater shrank.

She used too much bleach.

The blouse faded.

She mixed the white and dark clothes.

The white clothes turned pink.

It's not easy to care for clothes.

Write a story about a problem taking care of clothes.

One day I _____.

I used _____.

The _____.

Now _____.

1 2 3 4 5 6 7 8 9 10 11 12

What the Doctor Said ▪ ▪ ▪ ▪ ▪ ▪

Checkups

What's going on?
What are they thinking?

Kim and Joon wanted to have a baby. They wanted to have a brother or sister for their son, Han. They are very happy because Kim is pregnant. Naturally they want to have a healthy baby, so Kim sees the doctor often for checkups. These checkups are an important part of prenatal care.

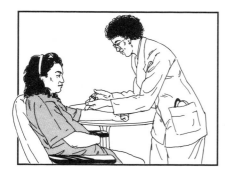  

First, a nurse weighs Kim. Then she takes her blood pressure. She takes a blood sample too. The doctor listens to the baby's heart, and then she lets Kim listen too. After the checkup, the doctor talks to both Kim and Joon. She asks them if they have any questions.

Think and talk about the questions.

1. Why is Kim having prenatal care?

2. Do you think it's a good idea?

3. Do you think it's important for men to learn about prenatal care?

4. Is there prenatal care in your native country?

A Medical History

A. Finish Kim's form.

Patient's name:				8/23/94
Lee	kim		Kang	
Last	First	Middle	Maiden	Today's date

General Health: ☑ Excellent ☐ Good ☐ Fair ☐ Poor

Height: __5'3"__ Weight: __132__

Do you smoke? ☐ Yes ☑ No If yes, how many packs a week? _____

Do you drink alcohol? ☐ Yes ☑ No If yes, how many glasses a week? _____

Check all that apply.	You	List family member(s)
High blood pressure	☐	
Heart problems	☐	
Diabetes	☐	
Tuberculosis	☐	
Anemia	☐	
Operations	☐	

Do you take any medication? (Include aspirin, eye drops, and over-the-counter drugs.)

Drug name	Dose	Reason

Are you allergic to any medication? If yes, list:

_____

_____

_____

B. What's your medical history?

1. Diseases _____

2. Medications _____

3. Operations _____

4. Allergies _____

| alcohol | blood | breakfast |
| caffeine | iron | weight |

Complete the sentences.

1. A _____ test showed that Kim is anemic.

2. The doctor wants Kim to take extra _____.

3. Kim's _____ and blood pressure are normal.

4. _____ is bad for babies. Kim doesn't drink it.

5. She doesn't drink coffee or tea now, either. They have _____.

6. Kim will take her pill with _____.

Olga wasn't feeling quite right, but she didn't really feel sick either. She went to see the doctor. She wanted to know if something was wrong. Olga's doctor examined her. He discovered that her blood pressure was high. He made some suggestions to help her feel better.

Underline the things that the doctor says Olga should do.

wear glasses	lose weight	run every day
eat fish	take aspirin	exercise
stop smoking	meditate	see a dentist
use less salt	reduce stress	take medication

Olga's on a diet. She's trying to lose some weight. She's paying more attention to the foods she eats, and she's trying to plan healthy meals.

A. Every day Olga can eat some of the following foods. Add more to the list.

Protein (5 servings)
meat   fish   eggs

_____
_____
_____

Fruit (4 servings)
apples   bananas

_____
_____
_____

Fats (3 servings)
oils   nuts   olives

_____
_____
_____

Starch (5 servings)
bread   cereal   rice

_____
_____
_____

Vegetables (3 or more servings)
asparagus   beets   carrots

_____
_____
_____

Dairy (2 servings)
milk   yogurt   cheese

_____
_____
_____

B. Plan a healthy menu for Olga.

Breakfast	Lunch	Snack	Dinner

What Causes Stress?

Olga's doctor wants her to reduce stress.
Stress can make you sick.

A. What causes stress for you?

B. Read this list. Check anything that happened to you in the last 12 months.

- ☐ 1. death in the family
- ☐ 2. marriage or divorce
- ☐ 3. pregnancy
- ☐ 4. a new family member
- ☐ 5. getting hired or fired from a job
- ☐ 6. spouse getting hired or fired from a job
- ☐ 7. moving
- ☐ 8. son or daughter leaving home
- ☐ 9. trouble in the family or with in-laws
- ☐ 10. winning special recognition or an award
- ☐ 11. _____
- ☐ 12. _____

C. Think and talk about the questions.

1. Did you check many events?
2. Do you think your life is stressful?
3. What do you think you can do to reduce stress?

Olga isn't sleeping very well. She often has an upset stomach or a headache. She is always thinking about her problems. She is constantly worrying about her sister's family. She even worries about all the people at Seacoast Industries. Olga is a considerate person; she is always trying to help other people.

A. What should Olga do to deal with her stress?

B. People do different things to deal with stress. What do you do?

Do you deal with stress by . . .

	Always	Sometimes	Never
1. smoking?			
2. drinking alcohol?			
3. meditating?			
4. exercising?			
5. taking medication?			
6. sleeping a lot?			
7. talking with someone?			
8. eating?			
9.			
10.			

Breaking Bad Habits

Olga wants to stop smoking.

First she tried eating candy. She gained weight.

Next she tried exercising. She was always hungry and sore.

Next she tried chewing gum. She got a cavity in her tooth.

Now she's in a support group. The members of the group are helping each other stop smoking. When Olga wants to smoke, she talks to someone in her group instead of smoking. She hasn't smoked for three weeks.

Write the answers.

1. What are some other bad habits? _____

_____

2. How could someone break them? _____

_____

_____

A. Put these pictures in order. Write the numbers.

B. Write sentences about the pictures.

1. _____

2. _____

3. _____

4. _____

5. _____

6. _____

C. Think and talk about the questions.

1. How do you think Kim and Joon feel?

2. How do you think Han feels?

Making the Connection

Olga was overweight and had high blood pressure. She was under stress. She went to see her doctor. He told her to lose weight, stop smoking, and exercise. He told her to relax. He gave her some medication too.

Six months later Olga went back to her doctor. She stopped smoking and she still lost 12 pounds. She walks home from work every day. Sometimes she walks to work too. She takes her medication, and her blood pressure is down. She feels healthier.

*What about **you**?*
    What are some medical problems you've had?
    What did you do?
    Have you ever been under stress?
    What did you do about it?

Write a story about yourself.

I was _____

_____

_____.

Then I _____

_____

_____.

Now I'm _____

_____

_____

_____.

1 2 3 4 5 6 7 8 9 10 11 12

Going to School ■ ■ ■ ■ ■ ■ ■ ■

At School

What's going on?
Why isn't Han reading?
Why is Johnny happy?
What are Isabel and Olga doing?

Han Lee's Class

Han Lee is in a class with children from many countries. His teacher is Ms. Hunter. She teaches second grade. She loves teaching so many different children.

Some of Han's classmates are learning English and some already know English.

Han sits at a table with three other children. Han's best friend is Arturo, who is from Mexico.

The other children at Han's table are Yolanda and Amy. Yolanda is from the Philippines and Amy is from the United States. Han, Arturo, and Yolanda also go to an ESL class together. They're learning English very quickly.

Han speaks English at school. He speaks Korean with his parents at home. Ms. Hunter thinks that's a good idea. She also likes her students to learn about other countries and cultures.

Think and talk about the questions.

1. Do you agree with Ms. Hunter? Why or why not?

2. What language do you speak at home?

3. How can children learn about other cultures?

Dear Parents,

Welcome to District 5 Elementary School! Our student enrollment is 350 children in Kindergarten through Grade 6. Most grades have two classes. Most classes have 20–25 children. Each class has one teacher. Some classes have a teacher's aide too. There are also teachers for art, music, gym, and special education.

All of our teachers want your child to have the best chance to grow in knowledge, in friendship, and in safety. I hope this handbook will be useful to you.

I look forward to working with you and your child during the school year.

Sincerely,

K. D. Smith

K. D. Smith
Principal

Where can you find out . . .

1. how your child should behave in school? Student Conduct, page 3

2. what the school holidays are? _____

3. what your third grader is studying? _____

4. what activities children can do after 3 p.m.? _____

5. who the kindergarten teacher is? _____

6. how your child can get to school? _____

A Note from School

District 5 Elementary School
1090 Valley Avenue
Westland, California 90600
(310) 555-9181

November 5, 1994

Dear Mr. and Mrs. Lee,

    I would like to meet with you to discuss Han's schoolwork. Han has been a very good student this year. However, he has changed recently. Now he doesn't turn in his homework. He's become very quiet in class. He failed a math quiz and two spelling tests in the last two weeks.

    I am in my classroom on Tuesdays and Wednesdays from 3:30 to 4:30 for parent conferences. Please come on either day.

Sincerely,

Lizette Hunter

Lizette Hunter
Second grade teacher

    Joon Lee works from 8 a.m. to 4 p.m. every day. He just started a new shift at Seacoast Industries. He can't miss work.

    Kim must take care of the new baby. The baby is sick, so she can't take her out of the house.

    They can't go to the meeting. They wonder what they should do.

What do you think they should do?

_____

_____

_____

Answer the questions.

1. How can Joon and Kim spend more time with Han? _____

   _____

   _____

2. Can you think of more ways? _____

   _____

   _____

High School Years

When Johnny Martino was in elementary school, he had only one teacher. He knew the teacher and the teacher knew him. He liked that. When he went to middle school, everything changed. He and his classmates had different teachers for different classes. They had to change classrooms every hour.

Now Johnny is in high school. He still has a lot of different teachers, and he and his friends have different schedules. It took Johnny a long time to get used to such a big school, and he wasn't so sure that he would like it. But he likes it now. There is more to high school than just taking classes. Johnny plays basketball for the Westland team, and he also takes photographs for the school newspaper. He is learning a lot in his classes, and he is learning a lot about himself.

Think and talk about the questions.

1. What are schools like in your native country?
2. How are schools different in the United States?

Johnny entered an essay contest and won. Here is his essay.

The Teacher I Admire Most
by John J. Martino

My mother died the year I was a freshman. I was in shock. I thought I'd never be happy again. I wanted to leave school. Everything in my life was wrong. I didn't even want to talk to my Dad. He was in shock like me.

Then I met Mr. Akiba. Mr. Akiba is the American History teacher. He's also my school counselor. We talked and he said, "You want to leave school? Of course, you may. Just help me understand why."

That sentence grabbed me. It showed me that he really cared. It made me deal with things I didn't want to think about. But Mr. Akiba was always with me. He kept talking to me and asking questions until he understood. By then, I understood too.

Mr. Akiba knows when to be quiet and when to yell. He knows when to be serious and when to joke. He even knows when to tell you to get lost. And he knows how to help you understand yourself too.

What more can a teacher do?

Think and talk about the questions.

1. Describe Mr. Akiba. What's he like?

2. Who do you talk to when you have problems?

3. What do you think makes a teacher or counselor special?

Adult Education Courses

Most school systems have courses for adults. Adults go to school for a lot of different reasons. Here are the adult education courses offered at one school.

	Monday	Tuesday	Wednesday	Thursday
6 p.m.	▸ ESL ▸ Spanish ▸ Résumé Writing	▸ Piano ▸ Perfect Pasta ▸ Typing	▸ ESL	▸ ESL ▸ Gentle Exercise ▸ Yoga
7 p.m.	▸ Auto Repair ▸ Dressmaking ▸ Tex-Mex Cooking	▸ Thai Cooking ▸ Bookkeeping	▸ Printmaking ▸ Aerobics ▸ Baking Breads	▸ American History ▸ Healthy Desserts
8 p.m.	▸ Stress Management ▸ Job Interview Workshop ▸ Business Writing	▸ H.S. Math ▸ H.S. Civics ▸ Computers I	▸ Pottery ▸ Guitar ▸ Computers II	▸ Quilting ▸ African Dance

Put the courses into categories.

Languages & Adult Basic Education (ABE)	Arts, Crafts, & Skills	Cooking	Business & Careers	Health, Exercise, & Dance
ESL	Auto Repair	Baking Breads	Typing	Yoga

At Registration

Register for
Night Classes
Now!

A. Choose the correct sentence in each pair.

1. _____ Isabel is signing up for American Civics.

   _____ Isabel is signing up for American History.

2. _____ Olga's doctor suggested that she take a yoga class.

   _____ Olga's doctor suggested that she learn how to make better pasta.

3. _____ Olga's yoga class is on Thursday at 6:00 p.m.

   _____ Isabel doesn't want to learn yoga.

4. _____ Althea is taking a class with Monroe.

   _____ Monroe is taking a cooking class.

5. _____ Isabel will not continue taking classes after she becomes a citizen.

   _____ Isabel enjoys taking adult education classes.

B. Think and talk about the questions.

1. What would you like to learn? Why?

2. What classes can you take? Where can you take them?

Adult Education

BUSINESS

Computers I   **Tuesday   8:00–9:00**

Learn all the basics of how computers work. No previous computer experience is necessary, but knowledge of the keyboard or typing is recommended. You will interact one-on-one with a computer!

COOKING

Baking Breads   **Wednesday   7:00–8:00**

Learn the art and techniques of baking all kinds of breads: white, rye, wheat, and fruit breads. The instructor will demonstrate and provide hands-on practice making, kneading, and rolling yeast dough. All supplies included. Bring an apron, though!

LANGUAGES

ESL (English as a Second Language)   **Monday   6:00–7:00**

This course is for people whose native language is not English and who have very little knowledge of English. The instructor will teach grammar and pronunciation basics and provide many opportunities for conversation. Buy your ESL textbook at the school bookstore before the first class.

HEALTH, EXERCISE, & DANCE

Yoga   **Thursday   6:00–7:00**

This is a six-session course consisting of practical, gentle exercises for men and women of all ages. Yoga makes you healthier and more physically fit, reduces stress, and raises energy levels. Wear loose-fitting clothing and bring an exercise mat to class.

Complete the sentences.

1. If you take the computer class, then you need to know _____
_____.

2. If you take the ESL class, then you will learn _____
_____.

3. If you take the yoga class, then you must wear _____
_____ and bring _____.

4. If you take the Baking Breads class, then you will practice _____
_____.

5. If you take the ESL class, then you must buy _____
_____.

People go to school for different reasons. Some people need to take classes to help them at work. Some people take classes to learn new things. And some people take classes to relax, have fun, and meet other people.

Write about why *you* take classes.

_____

_____

_____

_____

_____

_____

_____

_____

_____

_____

_____

_____

1 2 3 4 5 6 7 8 9 10 11 12
Becoming a Citizen ■ ■ ■ ■ ■ ■

Citizenship

What's going on?
What are they learning in class?
How do these people feel?

Isabel Santos came to the United States 10 years ago. She came because she couldn't find work in her country. Isabel got a job here. She also went to school to become a U.S. citizen. At first Isabel wasn't sure she wanted to be a U.S. citizen. She thought things might change in El Salvador. But then Isabel began to love the United States. She was proud to live here and wanted to become a citizen.

Stefan Zolonski came to the United States six years ago. He wasn't happy in Poland. He thought life in the United States was better for him. Some of his Polish friends remained permanent residents of the United States. They wanted to return to Poland. But Stefan wanted to stay in this country. He wanted to become a citizen.

Think and talk about the questions.

1. When did you come to the United States?

2. Why did you come here?

3. How are things different here from your native country?

What You Need to Become a Citizen

To become a citizen, you must:

1. be 18 years or older.
2. speak, read, and write English.
3. have good moral character.
4. be a permanent resident (have a Permanent Resident Card).
5. live in the United States as a permanent resident for five years.
6. know about United States history and government.

To become a citizen, you must also fill out an application, and you must send the INS:

1. two recent color photographs.
2. a completed Application for Naturalization (Form N-400).
3. a check or money order for $250. (This includes the $25 fee for fingerprinting.)
4. a photocopy of your Permanent Resident Card (front and back).

Don't send: your original Permanent Resident Card.

Circle the things you need to apply for citizenship.

a driver's license	a fingerprint form	a family photograph
a birth certificate	your passport	a $250 money order
two recent photographs	an Application for Naturalization form	a Permanent Resident Card

A. Interview.

	Isabel	Stefan	Joon			
18 or older?	✓	✓	✓			
Know English?	✓	✓	✓			
Know U.S. government and history?	✓	✓				
In U.S. five years?	✓	✓				
Permanent Resident?	✓	✓	✓			
Ready?	yes	yes	no			

B. Think and talk about the questions.

1. Why do many people want to become U.S. citizens?
2. Why do other people prefer to be permanent residents?
3. What can citizens do that permanent residents can't do?

Application for Naturalization

This block for government use only.

1. Your current legal name

   _____

2. Your name exactly as it appears on your Permanent Resident Card (if different from above)

   _____

3. Your Alien Registration ("A") Number

   _____

4. Your Social Security Number

   _____

5. Any other names you have used (including maiden name)

   _____

6. Your country of birth   Your country of nationality

   _____

7. Can you read and write English?   ☐ Yes   ☐ No

   _____

8. Can you speak English?   ☐ Yes   ☐ No

   _____

9. Can you pass a U.S. history and government test?   ☐ Yes   ☐ No

   _____

10. How many trips have you taken outside the U.S. since you became a permanent resident?

   _____

11. Have you served in the United States Armed Forces?   ☐ Yes   ☐ No

   _____

12. Branch of service

   _____

13. Type of discharge (honorable, dishonorable, etc.)

   _____

You may change your name when you become a U.S. citizen. If you want to do so, please print that name below.

Family Name (Last Name) _____

Given Name (First Name) _____

Isabel and Stefan must learn about American history. They are taking a history class. Listen to their teacher talk about American history.

Write the answers.

1. How many colonies were there? _____

2. What country owned the colonies? _____

3. Why did the colonists fight in the Revolution? _____
_____

4. Why was George Washington called the "Father of Our Country"?
_____

5. What did Thomas Jefferson write? _____

6. When is Independence Day? _____

The United States Government

The United States government has three branches.
The three branches have equal power.

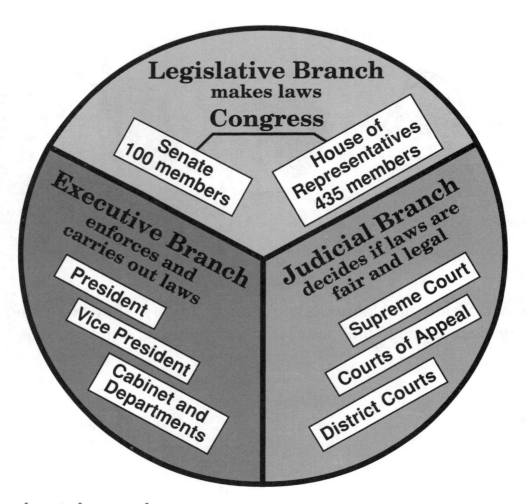

Choose the right word.

1. The _____ branch is the court system.
   (legislative/judicial)

2. The _____ has two representatives
   (Senate/House of Representatives)   from each state.

3. The _____ carries out the laws.
   (President/Senate)

4. The _____ branch makes laws.
   (legislative/judicial)

Here are some of the duties of U.S. citizens.

U.S. citizens . . .	Reasons
1. must obey laws.	1. Laws make people safe. People must know and respect the laws.
2. can vote for representatives.	2. U.S. citizens vote for their leaders of towns, cities, and states in local elections. They vote for president every four years in national elections too.
3. must pay taxes.	3. People pay taxes to the government. Taxes pay for things that everyone needs, like schools, roads, parks, and the military.

Think and talk about the questions.

1. Name some laws that you know.

2. U.S. citizens can change laws they disagree with. What laws do you think should be changed?

3. Why do people pay taxes in the United States?

4. Do people pay taxes in your native country?

5. Do most people vote in your native country?

6. Do you think it is important to vote? Why or why not?

Before the Interview

A. Check. ✔

	True	False
1. Isabel is worried about her job.		
2. Tony became a citizen almost 25 years ago.		
3. Tony came here alone.		
4. Tony never missed his country.		
5. Isabel misses her family and friends.		
6. Isabel wants to become a teacher.		

B. Think and talk about the questions.

1. Why do you think Isabel is nervous?
2. Do you ever get nervous? If so, why?

Isabel is at the Immigration and Naturalization Service office.
She is taking her citizenship test.

A. Match.

1. Declaration of Independence   **a.** Francis Scott Key

2. Civil War   **b.** Thomas Jefferson

3. "The Star-Spangled Banner"   **c.** Martin Luther King, Jr.

4. Civil Rights   **d.** Abraham Lincoln

B. Think and talk about the questions.

1. Did you know the answers?
2. Can you think of other questions that the examiner might ask?

Making the Connection

Isabel Santos was born in El Salvador. She came to the United States with her sister and brother. Her mother and father still live there and she writes to them often. Isabel is a U.S. citizen now. She can vote, and she knows and respects the law. It took Isabel many years to become a citizen. She's happy and proud.

Write your story.

Here are some questions to help you.

- What country did you come from?

- Who did you come with?

- Do you still have family or friends in your country?

- Do you want to go back?

- Do you want to become a U.S. citizen?

- How long do you think it will take you to become a citizen?

_____

_____

_____

_____

_____

_____

_____

_____

1 2 3 4 5 6 7 8 9 10 11 12
Getting Used to a New Land ■ ■ ■ ■

Arriving in a New Land

What's going on?
How do you think Olga and Isabel felt?
How do you think they feel now?
How did you feel when you arrived in the United States?
How do you feel now?

Ellis Island

Olga Kovacs and her family came to the United States from Hungary. Olga recently visited Ellis Island.

Ellis Island is an island in New York harbor. It has a long history.

From 1892 until 1954, it was the first stop in America for more than 17 million immigrants.

Immigrants waited in long lines. They were examined by doctors and questioned by inspectors.

The busiest year was 1907. More than one million immigrants passed through the "Gateway to America."

To honor all immigrants to this country, Ellis Island is now part of the Statue of Liberty National Monument.

Think and talk about the questions.

1. Have you seen the Statue of Liberty or Ellis Island?
2. How did you come to the United States?
3. Where did you enter the United States?
4. Did you have any trouble entering the United States?

A. Write the answers.

1. Why did Olga's parents come here? _____

_____

_____

2. What kind of job did Olga's father expect to get in the United States?

_____

_____

3. What did Isabel's cousin tell her about traveling? _____

_____

_____

4. How do Olga and Isabel feel about coming to the United States?

_____

_____

B. Think and talk about the questions.

1. Is the United States like you expected it to be?
2. If not, how is it different?
3. What surprised you the most about the United States?

Making Mistakes

When many people come to the United States, they don't know how to speak much English. They don't feel comfortable speaking the language. They don't feel comfortable with the customs either. They make a lot of mistakes.

Isabel moved to the United States when she was a teenager. She got lost all the time. She was afraid to ask for directions. She walked all over town. She hoped that she would see something familiar. Often she would cry because she missed her country. She never had these kinds of problems there.

Olga remembers that her parents didn't know how to open a bank account. They kept their money in the house. They were always afraid that someone would steal it. When Olga grew older and understood more, she took her parents to the bank and helped them open a bank account.

There are a lot of confusing things about the United States. People don't always act the same way as people from other countries. There is a lot to learn and it's not always easy.

A. Check. ✔

		True	False
1.	Many people make mistakes when they come to the United States.		
2.	Many people speak English when they come to the United States.		
3.	Isabel didn't need to ask for directions.		
4.	Olga's parents kept their money at home.		
5.	The United States is a confusing place.		

B. Think and talk about the questions.

1. When you first came to the United States, were you afraid or confused?
2. What are some things that were confusing to you?
3. What are some ways that people can learn about life in the United States?

Where is the _____?

bank
supermarket
post office

Kim and Joon Lee feel like they left Korea a long time ago. They only moved to the United States two years ago. Recently they learned it will take them three more years to become citizens. It seems a long time to them, but they think it will be worth the wait.

Kim and Joon don't feel at home in the United States yet, but they are quickly getting used to their new country. They don't want to return to Korea. They think that the United States is a good place to raise their family.

The Lees have already learned a lot of English. They take English classes when they have the time. They plan to take citizenship classes in the future.

| still | already | only | yet | recently |

Choose the correct word.

1. Joon and Kim are not U.S. citizens _____.

2. They're _____ not used to the United States.

3. They've _____ lived in the United States for two years.

4. _____ they learned they must wait to become U.S. citizens.

5. Kim and Joon _____ know a lot of English.

Feeling Foolish

Joon recently had an embarrassing experience.
He didn't know what to do or say.

Think and talk about the questions.

1. How did Joon feel?
2. How would you feel?
3. What do you think Joon did?
4. What would you do?

Monroe made an embarrassing mistake too.

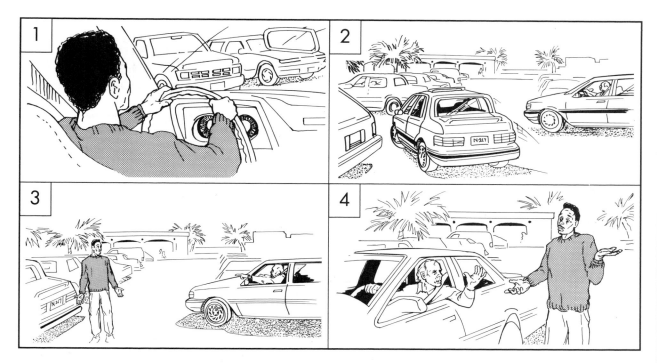

A. Write sentences about the pictures.

1. _____.

2. _____.

3. _____.

4. _____.

B. Think and talk about the questions.

1. If you ever have an embarrassing experience like Monroe's, what would you say or do?

2. How do you feel when you make mistakes in front of strangers? What about in front of friends?

Stereotypes

When Joon Lee came to the United States, he thought all Americans were selfish, loud, and very rude. After a while he met more and more Americans and discovered that many of them were not selfish. In fact, many of them were very helpful and friendly. But Joon still thinks that some Americans are loud and rude.

independent	lonely	smart	love to win
selfish	hardworking	rude	honest
unfriendly	don't care about others	hate to lose	loud
_____	_____	_____	_____

Interview.

When you came here, what did you think Americans were like? Now what do you think they are like? Use the words above or add your own words.

Name/Country	Then	Now
1. Isabel / El Salvador	rich, energetic, cold, hate to lose	hardworking, competitive, cold
2. _____ / _____		
3. _____ / _____		
4. _____ / _____		
5. _____ / _____		

Check. ✔

In your family, who . . .	In Your Native Country		In the United States	
	Men	**Women**	**Men**	**Women**
1. cooks the food?				
2. cleans the house?				
3. shops for groceries?				
4. decides how to spend money?				
5. takes care of babies?				
6. works outside the home?				
7. helps children with homework?				
8. fixes things around the house?				
9. _____ ?				
10. _____ ?				
11. _____ ?				
12. _____ ?				

A Different Kind of Life

Kim Lee thinks a lot about becoming a citizen of the United States. She's happy to be in the United States, but her life is very different from her life in Korea. There is so much to learn. Sometimes Kim feels stupid because she doesn't know very much about life in the United States. But she is learning! She's happy that her children will grow up in the United States. She wants the best for her family, and she's sure that the United States is the best place for them to live.

Kim writes to her sister, Soo Kang, every week. Soo Kang is studying business in Korea, and she is thinking of moving to the United States. Kim tells her that women have more freedom in the United States. They also can get better jobs in business than women in Korea. Kim says that in the United States women can often be the boss. Soo Kang thinks this is exciting. It isn't like that in Korea. Kim hopes that Soo Kang will move to the United States soon.

Think and talk about the questions.

1. Is life different for men than it is for women in your native country?
2. How is it different?
3. Do you like the difference or not?

A. Read Kim's story again.

B. Write a story about *your* life in the United States.

Here are some questions to help you.

- How do you feel about living in the United States?
- What do you like about it?
- What don't you like about it?
- Do you think men and women are treated the same?
- Do you think they should be?
- Would you want a younger sister or brother to live here?

_____

_____

_____

_____

_____

_____

_____

_____

_____

_____

_____

_____

_____

_____

_____

_____

Verbs: Future–*Going to* and *Will*

I	am (am not, 'm not)			I		
He		**going to**	<u>call</u> tonight.	He	**will ('ll)**	<u>call</u> tonight.
She	**is (is not, isn't)**			She		
It		**going to**	<u>start</u> at 8:00.	It	**will (will not)**	<u>start</u> at 8:00.
You				You		
We	**are (are not, aren't)**	**going to**	<u>study</u> tomorrow.	We	**will not (won't)**	<u>study</u> tomorrow.
They				They		

Is Olga **going to** <u>see</u> a doctor about that? She's **going to** <u>have</u> a checkup tomorrow.
Will you <u>be</u> at the party on Saturday? No, we **won't** <u>be</u> there.
When **will** Kim and Joon <u>talk</u> to Han's teacher? They**'ll** <u>go</u> to the school Monday.

A. Complete the sentences. Use *going to* or *will*.

Example: *Johnny:* "I _____ start school next week."
or: "I _____ start school next week."

1. *Aunt Tessa:* "So you_____ be in twelfth grade in September!"

2. *Johnny:* "That's right. I _____ be a senior. I think
we _____ have a great basketball team this year."

3. *Aunt Tessa:* "That's good. What about your classes? What classes are
you _____ take?"

4. *Johnny:* "The usual. English, math . . . Hey, Dad, _____ you let me
drive to school?"

5. *Tony:* "What? Well, we _____ see about that."

B. Answer the questions. Use either *going to* or *will*.

1. Is Olga going to take another exercise class?

No, she _____ take square dancing instead.

2. Will Kim and Joon sign up for evening classes?

No, not this time. They _____ spend more time with Han.

3. When will you start classes?

I _____ start in two weeks.

If you **can come,**	(then)	**let** me know.
If you **don't know** the answer,	(then)	you should **tell** the teacher.
If it **rains** tomorrow,	(then)	I**'m not going to** the picnic.
If Olga **doesn't finish** on time,	(then)	she **'ll miss** her bus home.
If Tony and Johnny **catch** a fish,	(then)	they **can eat** it for dinner.

A. Match.

1. *Tony:* "If I lift heavy boxes at work,

a. if you aren't careful."

2. *Doctor:* "If your back hurts,

b. if my back hurts?"

3. *Tony:* "But if I rest,

c. my back hurts."

4. *Doctor:* "Your back problems will get worse

d. you should stop and rest."

5. *Tony:* "Well, is there anything else I can do

e. if you need to lift something heavy."

6. *Doctor:* "Remember to bend your knees

f. who will do the work?"

B. Complete each sentence with the correct form of the word in parentheses. Add *will* or *should* if necessary.

If I _____ (be) better tomorrow, I _____

_____ (come) to work. If my back still _____

(hurt), I _____ (stay) in bed.

My doctor said that if I _____ (have) pain, then

I _____ (take) some medicine.

He also said that if I _____ (do) my exercises, my

back _____ (get) better.

Verb + infinitive
Stefan **plans to take** a trip to New York.
Kim and Joon **hope to become** citizens.
Isabel **decided to take** the test next week.
Don't **forget to write**.

Verb + *-ing*
Isabel **enjoys singing**.
Olga **quit smoking**.
Please **stop making** that noise.
Did you **finish studying**?

Verb + *-ing or infinitive*
Han **likes playing/to play** with his sister.
When did you **start exercising/to exercise**?
We **tried calling/to call** you last night.
They **hate doing/to do** housework.
But they **love having/to have** a clean house.

A. Underline the correct form.

1. The Bonners were planning **to go/going** to a wedding.

2. They needed **to buy/buying** a new suit for Monroe.

3. They kept **to look/looking** all afternoon.

4. Althea hoped **to get/getting** Monroe a shirt that would be easy to take care of.

5. Althea does not enjoy **to iron/ironing**.

6. Jody started **to get/getting** tired.

7. She wanted **to look/looking** at records.

8. Monroe almost forgot **to buy/buying** a new tie.

B. Fill in the correct form of the word in parentheses. Use *to* or *-ing*.

1. *Ramón:*   "We're trying _____ (start) a baseball team. What are you planning _____ (do) this Saturday?"

2. *Monroe:*   "I'd really love _____ (join) the team. But I need _____ (go) to a wedding with my family."

3. *Ramón:*   "So you can't come? We start at 8:00, so we'll finish _____ (play) at 11:00."

4. *Monroe:*   "Well, we won't be leaving until 1:00. I could try _____ (make) it Saturday morning. Where are you going to play?"

Ms. Hunter **feels that** Joon and Han **need** to help Kim more.
She also **thinks that** Han **is** a very good student.
Joon **told** Ms. Hunter **that** Kim **reads** to Han in Korean.

A. Complete the sentences, using *that.*

The nurse says:

Kim tells Joon:

1. "Monica looks healthy."

"The nurse thinks _____
_____."

2. "She has gained four pounds."

"The nurse told me _____
_____."

3. "Monica has a rash, though."

"The nurse is worried _____
_____."

4. "This medicine will help the rash."

"The nurse feels _____
_____."

5. "Everything else looks OK."

"The nurse thinks _____
_____."

6. "Monica is doing well."

"The nurse said _____
_____."

B. Complete the sentences, using *that.*

1. Kim says _____
_____
_____.

I want to be a good mother.

2. Tony thinks _____
_____
_____.

You are a good mother, Kim.

Tag Questions

Joon**'s** from Korea, **isn't** he?	Joon**'s not** a citizen yet, **is** he?
You**'re** feeling better, **aren't** you?	You**'re not** feeling well, **are** you?
She **speaks** Spanish, **doesn't** she?	She **doesn't** speak Italian, **does** she?
They **can** play here, **can't** they?	They **can't** play here, **can** they?
I **was** right, **wasn't** I?	I **wasn't** right, **was** I?
He **worked** here before, **didn't** he?	He **didn't** pass the test, **did** he?

A. Underline the correct tag questions.

1. The American flag has 50 stars, **doesn't it/does it**?

2. There aren't four branches of government, **aren't there/are there**?

3. You can become a citizen after five years, **can't you/can you**?

4. You don't need to send money, **don't you/do you**?

5. All citizens can vote, **can't they/can they**?

6. May 31 isn't Independence Day, **isn't it/is it**?

B. Complete each sentence with a tag question.

Stefan is helping Isabel study for her citizenship exam.

1. *Isabel:* "George Washington was the first president, _____?"

   Stefan: "Yes, that's right. And how many colonies were there?"

2. *Isabel:* "Let me think. There were 13 colonies, _____?"

   Stefan: "Right. Which branch of government makes the laws?"

3. *Isabel:* "Oh, dear. The legislative branch doesn't make them, _____?"

   Stefan: "Relax. You know the answers. Who was a black civil rights leader?"

4. *Isabel:* "That would be Martin Luther King, _____?"

   Stefan: "Right again."

5. *Isabel:* "I don't sound too nervous, _____?"

   Stefan: "Well, just a little. Don't worry. You'll do fine."

States and Their Standard Postal Abbreviations

Alabama	AL	Montana	MT
Alaska	AK	Nebraska	NE
Arizona	AZ	Nevada	NV
Arkansas	AR	New Hampshire	NH
California	CA	New Jersey	NJ
Colorado	CO	New Mexico	NM
Connecticut	CT	New York	NY
Delaware	DE	North Carolina	NC
Florida	FL	North Dakota	ND
Georgia	GA	Ohio	OH
Hawaii	HI	Oklahoma	OK
Idaho	ID	Oregon	OR
Illinois	IL	Pennsylvania	PA
Indiana	IN	Rhode Island	RI
Iowa	IA	South Carolina	SC
Kansas	KS	South Dakota	SD
Kentucky	KY	Tennessee	TN
Louisiana	LA	Texas	TX
Maine	ME	Utah	UT
Maryland	MD	Vermont	VT
Massachusetts	MA	Virginia	VA
Michigan	MI	Washington	WA
Minnesota	MN	West Virginia	WV
Mississippi	MS	Wisconsin	WI
Missouri	MO	Wyoming	WY

Other Postal Abbreviations

District of Columbia	DC	United States	US
Puerto Rico	PR	United States of America	USA

The United States of America

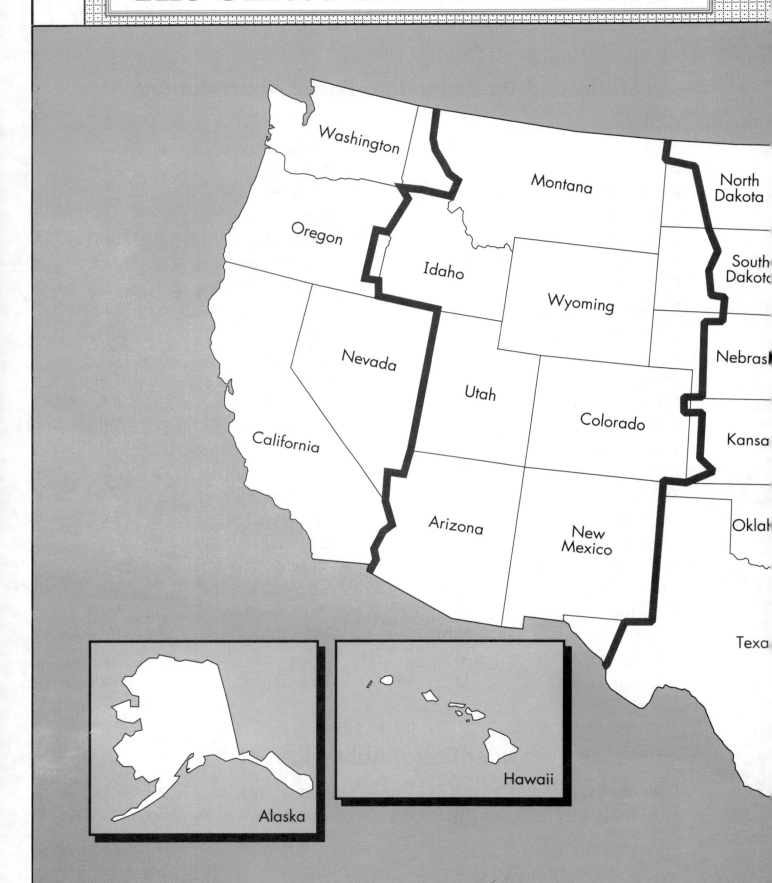

Washington

Oregon

Montana

North Dakota

Idaho

South Dakota

Wyoming

Nevada

Nebras

California

Utah

Colorado

Kansa

Arizona

New Mexico

Oklah

Texa

Alaska

Hawaii

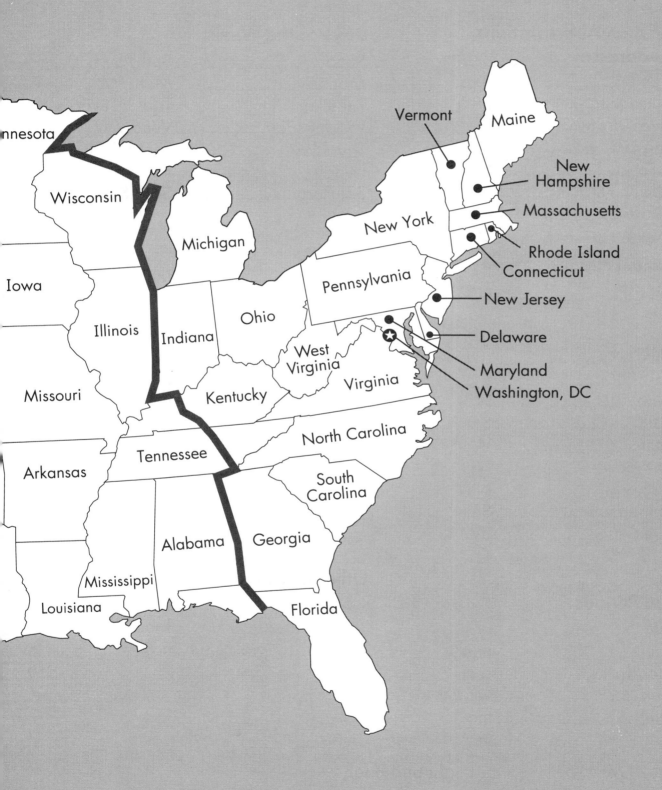

Common Abbreviations

Common Abbreviations in Addresses

Avenue	Ave.
Boulevard	Blvd.
Drive	Dr.
Lane	Ln.
Place	Pl.
Road	Rd.
Square	Sq.
Street	St.
Apartment	Apt.
Post Office	PO

Directions

East	E
North	N
South	S
West	W
Northeast	NE
Northwest	NW
Southeast	SE
Southwest	SW

Time Periods

hour	hr.
minute	min.
second	sec.
week	wk.
month	mo.
year	yr.

a.m./AM:	between midnight and noon
p.m./PM:	between noon and midnight

Days of the Week

Sunday	Sun./Su
Monday	Mon./M
Tuesday	Tues./Tu
Wednesday	Wed./W
Thursday	Thurs./Thu./Th
Friday	Fri./F
Saturday	Sat./S

Months

January	Jan.
February	Feb.
March	Mar.
April	Apr.
May	—
June	Jun.
July	Jul.
August	Aug.
September	Sept.
October	Oct.
November	Nov.
December	Dec.

Other Common Abbreviations

Company	Co.
Incorporated	Inc.
number	no.